I₀1₀5631

INTRODUCTION

I thank God for my wife. We have just celebrated fifty-five years of marriage. The Bible says, *"Whoso findeth a wife findeth a good thing, and obtaineth favor of the LORD."*[1] I found a good thing.

My father died when I was young and my mother, a widow with four children, remarried when I was in High School. She moved our family to Florida with her new husband, my beloved "Pop" where I met the treasure I later married.

My Pop was God sent to us. He dearly loved my mother and was so good to all her children. He taught me how to be a man, to work hard, and how to love and take care of my family.

I almost did not have a chance to convince Nancy, my sweet wife, to marry me. On one of our first dates, Nancy and I went somewhere with my mom and pop. My pop who was a fun-loving guy, said, "The fair is in town. Let's go to it." I said, "All right, let's go." So, we all went to the fair to ride some rides, and we rode several of them.

(1) Proverbs 18:22

★ ★ ★ ★ ★

I could tell I was starting to feel a little sick, and my head was spinning a little bit. I wanted to take a break from the rides and walk around.

Then my pop said, "I have never seen anyone swallow a sword. There is a little sideshow here where a woman swallows a sword. Let's go watch her."

My head was spinning a little more and I was feeling queasy from riding the rides, but I did not want anyone to know it, so I said, "Okay Pop, we'll go watch this woman swallow a sword."

We went in and, of course, my pop wanted to be right where the action was, so there we were, standing in the sawdust in the front row.

This woman took out a sword that looked as long as her arm and started swallowing it. I saw about four inches go down her throat and that was the last thing I remember. I was face down in the sawdust. People were calling paramedics and everything.

They thought I had a heart attack. I told Nancy, "I must have a touch of the flu. I am not that weak of a man." For all these years my wife still finds humor in telling her take on when I fainted on our first date. Her version is a little less manly.

I do not know why that girl ever married me, but I thank God she did. It is true, "Whoso findeth a wife findeth a good thing," even one who tells all the funny stories about you.

★ ★ ★ ★ ★

Marrying Right

A Guide To Choosing Life's Mate

Young people have three choices to make in life.

What will you do with Jesus?

What will you do with your life?

With whom will you spend the rest of your life?

The quality of one's life is determined by the quality of the decisions they make. This helpful book will guide young people to finding God's mate for life.

ISBN: 979-8-9905333-1-8

Dr. Tom Sexton

CHRISTIAN MINISTRIES

Marrying Right
SUBJECTS COVERED

God blessed our home with two precious daughters and now we have five grandchildren and four great grandchildren (we hope more are on their way). I thank God for His blessings on our family. The Bible says, *"I have no greater joy than to hear that my children walk in truth."*[2]

I pray every day that they will continue to live for the Lord and that God will keep a hedge of protection about them.

I am very much concerned about all my family members marrying right. Who people marry is one of the most important things in the world.

Three of the most important decisions young people make are:

1. **What will I do with Christ?**

2. **What will I do with my life?**

3. **With whom will I spend my life?**

God has a plan and a purpose for marriage. God has a great promise for a marriage if the marriage is right. *"For this cause shall a man leave his father and mother, and shall be joined unto his wife, and they two shall be one flesh. This is a great mystery: but I speak concerning Christ and the church."*[3]

Many people are very concerned about marrying the right person, that one person God wants them to marry, and they end up more confused than a termite in a yo-yo. God wants you to make sure you marry the right person, but sometimes just thinking about Mr. or Mrs. Right will get you in trouble, and you will miss the person God has for you.

Marrying right means more than just marrying the right person. God wants you to marry right, and He will help you identify the right person. Marrying right helps you know for sure that you are marrying the right person.

Some marry the right person, but go about it all wrong, and have a lifetime doubting whether they married the right person.

TRUST IS THE FOUNDATION OF A LOVING RELATIONSHIP

"Trust in Him at all times; ye people, pour out your heart before Him: God is a refuge for us."[4]

Before I give you the keys to unlocking the wisdom from the Bible, in finding the one person God has for you to marry, let me say a word about trust. Trust is the foundation of any loving relationship.

God wants you to make sure that you can trust someone before you give them your heart. The Bible says about Jesus, *"Trust in Him at all times; ye people, pour out your heart before Him: God is a refuge for us."*[5] We trust Him, that is why we give Him our heart and then He becomes our strength. First there must be trust.

Many times, a person gives their heart to someone they cannot trust. Once they fall in love with that person, they are in a heap of trouble, because they may miss marrying the right person.

Make sure that the person you are going to marry is someone you can trust – before you give them your heart. *"Keep thy heart with all diligence; for out of it are the issues of life."*[6]

In choosing life's mate, you must ask yourself, "How can I know that I am marrying the one God has chosen for me? How can I be sure they are the right one? Can I trust this person with my future?"

A Bride for Isaac

There is a wonderful example of finding the right person, someone you can trust, to spend your life with by following the principles in the Bible. We see how Isaac's wife was chosen. Abraham understood the three things' couples must have for a God blessed home.

They must be of the same **Faith**, fit in the **Family** and desire the same **Future**.

The Bible says, *"And Abraham was old, and well stricken in age: and the LORD had blessed Abraham in all things. And Abraham said unto his eldest servant...swear by the LORD, the God of heaven, and the God of the earth, that thou shalt not take a wife unto my son of the daughters of the Canaanites, among whom I dwell: But thou shalt go unto my country, and to my kindred, and take a wife unto my son Isaac.*

And Abraham said unto him...The LORD God of heaven, which took me from my father's house, and from the land of my kindred, and which spake unto me, and that sware unto me, saying, Unto thy seed will I give this land.

★ ★ ★ ★ ★

He shall send his angel before thee, and thou shalt take a wife unto my son from thence.

And if the woman will not be willing to follow thee, then thou shalt be clear from this my oath: only bring not my son thither again. And the servant...sware to him concerning that matter."[7]

Again, let me say, Abraham wanted a wife for his son who was of the same **Faith**, a wife who could fit in with the **Family**, and a wife who wanted the same **Future** as Isaac. That is the marriage every God-fearing father desires for their son or daughter.

I have made a list of five keys that will open the door of blessings to any couple who wishes to have God's best in marriage. These keys will help any serious-minded Christian know GOD's will in their marriage.

God will point out the right person for you if you follow these five principles.

Please The Lord with Your Relationship

"I do always those things that please Him"[8]

Marrying right means that you are willing to please God with your relationship. It means maintaining a good testimony with that person. Pleasing God is the highest goal in a Christian's life. It is the highest form of Christianity.

Jesus said, "He that sent Me is with Me: the Father hath not left Me alone; for I do always those things that please Him." (8) The Lord Jesus gave us by example, the highest goal for life. It is to please God.

Questions to ask about your relationship:

- Are you keeping yourselves right with God?

- Are you helping each other to be better Christians?

- Are you able to talk together about God's plan and purpose for your lives?

(8) John 8:29

★ ★ ★ ★ ★

- Are you living above reproach?

"Abstain from all appearance of evil."[9] Living above reproach means a young couple will not have to ask, "Who caught us?" Instead, they will be able to say, "No one can accuse us."

Parents should teach their children from an early age that the goal of life is to please the Lord. Then when children get to the age of choosing a mate, they have already established the highest goal of the Christian life.

When my daughters were young, a layman at Highland Park Baptist Church called me aside and said, "Brother Tom, teach your children to please God. That is all they have to do with their lives." I thank God for the wisdom that dear brother in the Lord gave me.

As my children were growing up, I told them, "Girls, I want you to do one thing: Just please the Lord with your lives, and your mom and dad are going to be so happy."

Think of all the problems children face growing up. I could simply say, "Sweetheart I do not think the way you handled that was pleasing to the Lord."

Please do not think our home did not have some of the same difficulties homes face today, but we did have a high goal for our relationships with ourselves and others. We wanted to please the Lord with our life and family. May I say there were times we really had to work at it.

(9) I Thessalonians 5:22

★ ★ ★ ★ ★

The Lord Jesus pleased God with His life, with His ministry, and with His death on Calvary. He pleased God. No wonder He could say, *"I do always those things that please Him."*[8]

Pleasing the Lord is the way every loving trusting relationship should begin. Marrying right means you are willing to please God with the person and the way in which you are going to marry.

Marrying right means that you are willing to please God in the private times together. The time you spend together should leave you closer to the Lord, with a stronger desire to be your best for God.

Pleasing God means that you do not open any wedding presents until the wedding night. God has some wonderful wedding presents, and He is not happy when you open them up before the wedding night.

- He gives a couple an intimate physical relationship.

This is a wonderful wedding present best kept wrapped until marriage. Times have changed, but the Bible is very clear about beginning an intimate relationship before marriage. He gives the bride a love she never experienced before marriage.

- God gives a bride the gift of undying love.

People say that they are getting married because they love each other. However, the love you have for your wife is not the same love you have for your girlfriend or fiancé.

It is not the same because the Bible says, *"Husbands, love your wives even as Christ also loved the church, and gave himself for it."*[10] Your bride is not your wife until you get married. God gives you, on your wedding day, a deeper, Christlike love for your wife. It is one of the presents God gives a Christian couple when they are joined together in holy matrimony and marry right.

When young people get involved in a relationship that is displeasing to the Lord, they will lack God's peace and blessing until they get things right with the Lord.

Beginning a physical intimate relationship before marriage will cause a lack of discernment in spiritual decision making.

Begin your relationship with a commitment to please the Lord and build your future on truth and trust. The Lord will give you His blessing in your home.

Marrying right means your relationship with the one you wish to marry is pleasing God.

(10) Ephesians 5:25

★ ★ ★ ★ ★

SEEK THE BLESSING OF YOUR PARENTS

Marrying right means that you are going to desire your parents' blessing on your marriage.

The Bible says, *"Children, obey your parents in the Lord: for this is right. Honor thy father and mother; which is the first commandment with promise; That it may be well with thee, and thou mayest live long on the earth."*[11]

Do you want it to go well? There are a lot of young people who have married, and it is not going well, because they did not consider what their parents thought about the person they married.

I know there is an age when the law of the land says you can make your own decisions about your life and marriage. But that does not mean we should leave the people who raised us, and who have invested their life in us, out of the process of choosing our life's mate.

Young people should be very interested in what their parents have to say about what they are going to do. Some

(11) Ephesians 6: 1-3

★ ★ ★ ★ ★

young people think that their parents have lost touch with life. What they have not learned is that people are people no matter what age or generation.

Whether the parents are saved or lost does not matter. Your parents know you better than anyone. They also know two things about you.

- Parents know the **type** of person you should marry.

Parents know you better than you think. Believe it or not, parents know the type of person you could be happy with. They want you to be loved, cherished, and happy in your marriage.

Parents may not be able to see into the future, but they have lived long enough to know people who are now living with decisions made in their youth.

They know marriage is not a "Fairytale" lived in a castle. It is for mature believers who have united for the amazing journey of life. A journey filled with precious memories, the joy of a loving family, friendships with likeminded people, and an undying love for the ages.

They do not want their "Cinderella" daughter to wake up and discover she kissed the wrong frog, and then over the years, becomes the wicked stepmother. They do not want their "Prince Charming" son to lose his charm, and over the years, turn into the evil king.

So, be wise enough to allow your parents to give some input into your choice of mate. They do know the type of person who will not change the sweet loving person you have become.

They know the type of person who will be a joy at birthday celebrations, at holidays, at family meals and other special times spent together with the entire family. They know who will "fit-in" around the family table.

Honor your parents and family with your choice. You will always have the support of the ones you care enough about, when you seek their blessing to marry their son or daughter.

They know what kind of woman is going to be a good wife for their son. Make sure your parents think the person you are going to marry will be a good mate for you.

- Parents know when it is **time** for you to marry.

Parents know the time that their children are ready to get married. The Bible says, *"When I was a child, I spake as a child, I understood as a child, I thought as a child: but when I became a man, I put away childish things."*[12] Parents know when boys become men, and when girls become women.

Daughters

Parents know if their daughter is ready for the responsibility of having a marriage, a family, and if they can guide the home. The Bible says, *"I will therefore that the younger women marry, bear children, guide the house, give no occasion to the adversary to speak reproachfully."*[13]

Women who marry, have children, take care of the home, and keep the devil from getting his foot in the door, have a big responsibility. The statement, "guide the home" in our text is a powerful truth every mother should teach their daughters.

Men lead the home, but women guide the home and create the spirit of the home. Homes need godly leadership, and the sweet spirit of a wise guide.

Parents know when their daughter is ready for this chapter of their life, and if she is ready to do her part in the marriage. Young men should not marry a girl if her parents do not believe she is ready to get married. It would be a big mistake to marry a woman with a bad spirit.

The bible says, *"It is better to dwell in a corner of the housetop, than with a brawling woman in a wide house. It is better to dwell in the wilderness, than with a contentious and an angry woman."*[14]

Sons

Parents know when their son is ready to leave home, provide for his family and lead the home. A husband must be a source of strength for his wife and children.

The Bible says to men, *"if any provide not for his own, and especially for those of his own house, he hath denied the faith, and is worse than an infidel."*[15]

If a young man's parents do not believe he is ready and mature enough to take a wife, then it would be a big mistake to marry him.

The Bible also says to men, *"Therefore shall a man **leave** his father and his mother and shall **cleave** unto his wife: and they shall be one flesh."*[16] I have never met a young wife who was happily married to a man who could not leave his parents.

Should a young man leave his home when he marries?

The Lord Jesus answered this question when He said, *"Have ye not read, that He which made them at the beginning made them male and female…And said, For this cause shall a man **leave** father and mother and shall **cleave** to his wife: and they twain shall be one flesh…Wherefore they are no more twain, but one flesh. What therefore God hath joined together, let no man put asunder."*[17]

Good men watch out for their family. Jesus said, *"But know this, that if the goodman of the house had known in what watch the thief would come, he would have watched, and would not have suffered his house to be broken up."*[18]

Fathers want their daughters to marry men who will keep them safe and protect them from harm.

(15) I Timothy 5:8 (16) Genesis 2:24 (17) Matthew 19: 4-6 (18) Matthew 24:43

★ ★ ★ ★ ★

If a man is not wise enough to protect his family; his wife and children may be at risk in our changing world. If a family is off track, it is the responsibility of the husband and father to fix it.

A woman should not marry a man whose family does not believe he is ready to lead his home. Men lead homes and women create the spirit in homes.

GET COUNSEL FROM SPIRITUAL LEADERSHIP

Marrying right means you will have your spiritual leadership's blessing.

"Obey them that have the rule over you, and submit yourselves: for they watch for your souls, as they must give account, that they may do it with joy, and not with grief: for that is unprofitable for you…Remember them which have the rule over you, who have spoken unto you the Word of God: whose faith follow, considering the end of their conversation."[19]

You may ask, "Why should I care what my pastor thinks about the person I want to marry?

- Jesus wants families to be together forever.

Jesus said He is preparing a home in Heaven for His children. He said, *"In my Father's house are many mansions: if it were not so, I would have told you. I go to prepare a place for you. And if I go and prepare a place for you, I will come again, and receive you unto myself; that where I am, there ye may be also."*[20]

(19) Hebrews 13:7,17 (20) John 14:2-3

★ ★ ★ ★ ★

I cannot imagine someone genuinely loving another human being, wanting to spend their life with them, and yet not wanting to spend their eternity with them. Do you want to spend forever with the people you love?

Forever With You

By Tom Sexton

It is you that makes my life worth living
With all its twists and all its turns
The love filled days that we have shared together
Is what my heart forever yearns
Yes, everyone lives somewhere forever
And one day we will see it is true
My forever would be so lonely
If your sweet love I never knew
Your love for me has never altered
No matter what we have gone through
And when my life's journey is over
I choose my forever to be with you
Yes, everyone will live their forever
Our hearts love will never die, 'tis true
That's why I'm choosing my forever
To be lived in Heaven with you

Can be sung to the tune "Danny Boy"

★ ★ ★ ★ ★

- Spiritual leadership knows if you are equally yoked.

The Bible says, *"Be ye not unequally yoked together with unbelievers: for what fellowship hath righteousness with unrighteousness? and what communion hath light with darkness?"*[21] To be *"unequally yoked"* means more than being saved or lost.

There are many couples who are both saved, but are not both surrendered to the Lord. It is bad enough to be married and not go to church faithfully, but when children come, the real battle begins.

When one parent wants to be faithful to the Lord and find their place of service in the church, and the other one wants to take their children to the lake on Sunday, there is trouble in the home.

- Spiritual leadership helps your marriage finish strong.

The Bible says, *"...let us run with patience the race that is set before us, Looking unto Jesus the author and finisher of our faith; who for the joy that was set before Him endured the cross, despising the shame, and is set down at the right hand of the throne of God"*[22]

Marriage is a new beginning in a couple's life. It is a celebration of two who have united for life. A joyful celebration for all who are present at the wedding. But what makes a marriage wonderful is the journey and the blessings enjoyed together.

The Bible says, *"Better is the end of a thing than the beginning thereof."*[23] I know that is hard to see for a young couple in love, but it is true. Young couples need help seeing the future, and the future is wonderful with couples who love each other and grow old together. Get your spiritual leaderships blessing. Get it right at the beginning and enjoy the journey.

"He that walketh with wise men shall be wise: but a companion of fools shall be destroyed."

Proverbs 13:20

★ ★ ★ ★ ★

SUPPORTED BY GOOD, GODLY FRIENDS

The Lord Jesus went to a wedding as a friend. His presence was a testimony for this couple. The Bible says, *"And the third day there was a marriage in Cana of Galilee; and the mother of Jesus was there: And both Jesus was called, and His disciples, to the marriage."*[24]

Jesus and the disciples were friends of the ones who were getting married, and their presence at the wedding was a testimony that they thought it was good.

Make sure your good Christian friends are supportive of your marriage. Now, I am not talking about your friends who are nonbelievers, or who are in rebellion. I am talking about the friends who know God and desire God's best for your life. Make sure those friends think it is good.

Everyone has some friends that want the best for them, friends that love them. Find out what they think about you two being a couple.

Your true friends know if you are good for each other. Put a lot of stock in the friends that know you and want God's best for your life. If they do not think it is good, find out why. The Bible says, *"A friend loveth at all times, and a brother is born for adversity."*[25]

Good friends will tell you the truth even when it hurts. The Bible says, *"Faithful are the wounds of a friend; but the kisses of an enemy are deceitful."*[26] If your Christian friends, that genuinely want God's best for you, think that this relationship is good, that is wonderful.

But if your best friends think you are making a mistake, you may be making a mistake. Remember, *"He that walketh with wise men shall be wise: but a companion of fools shall be destroyed."*[27] What do your good, godly friends think about it? Are they able to rejoice?

---

(25) Proverbs 17:17 (26) Proverbs 27:6 (27) Proverbs 13:20

★ ★ ★ ★ ★

MARRYING YOUR HEARTS DESIRE

We read in the Bible if we, *"Trust in the LORD, and do good"* and *"Delight…also in the LORD"* that *"He shall give thee the desires of thine heart…He shall bring it to pass."*[28]

The Lord promises that if we trust Him and commit our ways to Him, He will give us the desires of our hearts. This means if you are yielded to Christ, have kept your relationship right, and have followed the truth you have been given, He will increase your desire, if it is His will.

The Bible says, *"no **good** thing will He"* (The Lord) *"withhold from them that walk uprightly."*[29] And the Bible says, *"Whoso findeth a wife findeth a **good** thing, and obtaineth favour of the LORD."*[30]

The last principle to consider has to do with these questions: Is this what you truly desire? Do you really want to do this? Is this the person with whom you desire to spend the rest of your life?

(28) Psalm 37: 3-5   (29) Psalm 84:11   (30) Proverbs 18:22

★ ★ ★ ★ ★

Consider again the following areas:

Family.

Do you both agree on how your family is going to be? Are you in agreement about education for your children? Do you share the same convictions about celebrating holidays and special days as a family?

How important are children's needs going to be? How much involvement will your in-laws have in your marriage?

Spend some time before you marry with the families you are marrying into, especially around the holidays and birthdays. Families have traditions that are important to them. Make sure you both agree on how you plan to continue your families' traditions.

I have known young brides who believed they could change their husbands after marriage, but discovered that people are like the families they grew up in. It takes a work of grace to change a man or a woman.

Remember, Abraham told his servant to find a wife for Isaac that would fit in the family.

Faith.

What church are you going to attend together? How involved will you be as a family in the Lord's work? Have you, as a couple, strengthened each other's faith? Are you better

Christians today than before you met?

The Bible teaches us that the righteousness of God is "*revealed from faith to faith*."[31] In other words, we teach our children the things of God, and they in turn teach their children the same.

Future.

Is there a real future together? Are you both willing to make a long-term commitment? Will this marriage be for better or worse? In sickness and in health? For richer or poorer? Will this marriage last until death do you part?

These five powerful truths will help you choose life's mate. Make sure you are:

- Pleasing The Lord With Your Relationship.

- Seeking The Blessing of Your Parents.

- Getting Counsel From Spiritual Leadership

- Supported by Good, Godly Friends

- Marrying Your Hearts Desire

These five things will line up and point to the right person. If one of these things is out of line, do not move forward. Wait until the Lord gives you all five.[31]

"Be careful for nothing;

but in every thing by

prayer and supplication

with thanksgiving let your

requests be made known

unto God."

Philippians 4:6

★ ★ ★ ★ ★

Mistakes Often Made by Young Couples

1. Their relationship is based on the flesh. They look only at the physical and never know the real person. Get to Know the *"hidden man of the heart, in that which is not corruptible, even the ornament of a meek and quiet spirit, which is in the sight of God of great price."*[32]

2. They are slaves to second best. They never really wanted God's best in any area of their lives. The Lord wants to *"prove what is that good, and acceptable, and perfect, will of God."*[33] God will always give the best to them that leave the choice up to Him.

3. They think they must marry because they have so much time invested in this person. The Bible says *"...forgetting those things which are behind, and reaching forth unto those things which are before, I press toward the mark for the prize of the high calling of God in Christ Jesus."*[34]

4. They have gone too far physically and now feel marriage is the right thing to do. The Lord Jesus told the woman taken in adultery to *"Go, and sin no more."*[35]

(32) I Peter 1:4 (33) Romans 12:2 (34) Philippians 3:13,14 (35) John 8:2-11

★ ★ ★ ★ ★

These reasons are not pleasing to the Lord and will leave people questioning, all their lives, whether they married the right person. The Lord has promised to give us peace.

This peace is what every young person should have before marrying. The Bible says, *"Be careful for nothing; but in every thing by prayer and supplication with thanksgiving let your requests be made known unto God. And the peace of God, which passeth all understanding, shall keep your hearts and minds through Christ Jesus."*[36]

If there is any doubt about one or more of these areas, you should wait on God to give you peace.

AFTER THE WEDDING
WHAT'S NEXT

Imagine a young couple coming to a door that reads, "Enter to Marry." They knock on the door, and someone asks, "Are you ready to get married?" They answer, "Yes!"

The next question they hear is, "Tell us why you two believe you are ready for marriage." They say,

1. We have a relationship that has been pleasing and right with the Lord.

2. Our family believes we are right for each other.

3. Our pastor has counseled us and believes we are equally yoked.

4. Our Christian friends are supportive of us.

5. It is the desire of our hearts to marry each other.

They now go through the door of marriage and have a beautiful wedding. Family and friends rejoice with them. They

★ ★ ★ ★ ★

turn and look at the door they came through and it reads, "Have A Five Star Christian Marriage."

Now someone asks them this question, "Do you want to have a Five Star Christian Marriage?" They answer, "Yes how do we achieve it?" The answer comes, "Do these five things faithfully."

1. Keep things right with the Lord.

2. Stay in the spirit of one accord with your family.

3. Be faithful and active in church.

4. Develop good Christian friendships.

5. Put your whole heart into your marriage.

The five truths that gives you the peace to marry is the same truth you must build on to have a great marriage. They are the five pillars of the foundation for a Five Star Christian Marriage.

HAVE A FIVE STAR CHRISTIAN MARRIAGE

"What therefore God hath joined together, let not man put asunder."[37]

I like to remind the wedding party, at the rehearsal, that the wedding is for the Bride. This is her day. Let us all work together to make sure she has the desire of her heart on her wedding day. The marriage and the honeymoon will be the husband's reward for his making her day special.

I read a survey of couples, after five years of marriage, about the bride's take on her wedding, and marriage. I was shocked to read that the brides, who took the survey, said they experienced more joy and happiness in planning their weddings than they did from their marriages.

That article reminded me of a joke I heard that is funny, but if true is sad. A woman said, "I never knew what real happiness was until I got married. Then it was too late."

Every couple must remember that it will take the same love and commitment in their marriage, that it did to fall in love

(37) Matthew 19:1-8

★ ★ ★ ★ ★

and get married. Do not stop working on your relationship after you are married and get back from the honeymoon.

Couples get on the same page to get married, and they must stay on the same page in the marriage to make it golden.

I authored a poem I would like to share with you about the home my wife and I tried to provide for our children. I went to college later in life. My sweet wife and I both worked extremely hard going to college with two small children, schooling, jobs, and faithfully serving in our church.

Our house was very small, but our home was a place of refuge and I have such sweet memories from those days.

Is There a Home in *Your Marriage?*

Home is a place where young hearts are safe

It allows those we love to live and to share our space

Home is a place where kindness abounds

In our homes life's most valuable treasures are found

Home is a place where we travel back to in our minds

It is there golden moments are frozen in time

I would rather have a home and live in a tent

Than to reflect on a dwelling where my life was spent

What kind of marriage do you want to have? Do you want a marriage that stands the test of time?

Do you want a home filled with love that has the blessings of the Lord?

Do you want a family that will be the greatest treasure of your life?

Do you want your children to grow up with sweet memories of a home they treasure all their lives?

You can have that home. May I suggest having a "Five Star Christian Marriage"?

Keep Things Right With The Lord

"Except the LORD build the house, they labor in vain that build it."[38]

Let God work in your marriage and home. Keep the right relationship with each other, and the Lord. Keep your heart in tune with the Lord. The Bible says, *"If we confess our sins, He is faithful and just to forgive us our sins, and to cleanse us from all unrighteousness."*[39]

The highest goal in a Christian home is to please the Lord. Jesus said, *"I do always those things that please Him."*[40]

Stay In One Accord With Your Family

"Speaking to yourselves…Submitting yourselves one to another in the fear of God."[41]

Understand each other's differences. Learn how to talk things out. Communication is the life blood of a marriage.

Let me share with you some advice I gave a young husband when he had his first "Fuss-Fight" with his wife.

The Bible says, *"Death and life are in the power of the tongue."*[42] So, I told him, the next time you find yourself in a fuss-fight with your wife, here are three things you need to do.

1. **Surrender** the first opportunity you are given to speak. Remember it may be a while before she gives you an opportunity to say anything.

2. **'Keep Quiet'** if she accepts your surrender, while she gives you her closing statement and your conditions of surrender.

3. **Do not say another word,** even if you believe the final word is yours. Always remember anything you say at the end of what she says will be the beginning of a new argument and you will wish you had kept quiet.

Remember this Bible verse. *"Even a fool, when he holdeth his peace, is counted wise: and he that shutteth his lips is esteemed a man of understanding."*[43]

Learn the difference between the way women communicate and men communicate. Men sometimes talk in what I call "Headlines" they just speak in short statements.

Women talk in paragraphs, chapters, and sometimes books. And may I say, women love to ask questions, and follow up questions.

One dear old soul told me that by the time he learned how to read his wife, his library card had expired.

Be Faithful And Active In Church

Jesus told Peter to, *"strengthen thy brethren."*[44]

I remind couples that everyone needs three homes. They need a Heavenly home; they need a Christian home, and they need a church home. A Christian home gets strengthened by a good church home. Be faithful to church.

Develop Good Christian Friendships

"He that walketh with wise men shall be wise: but a companion of fools shall be destroyed…Iron sharpeneth iron; so, a man sharpeneth the countenance of his friend."[45]

Young couples need good Christian friends.

Put Your Whole Heart Into Your Marriage

"Husbands, love your wives, even as Christ also loved the church, and gave Himself for it…Husbands, love your wives, and be not bitter against them."[46]

Do not be halfhearted in your marriage. Ask the Lord to give you a deeper love for one another, and do not allow bitterness to get between you.

Do not try to find fault with one another, and guard against talking negative to others about your spouse. However, it is ok to talk to the Lord about everything.

One young wife had the habit of writing her heart talks out to the Lord in her diary. Her husband said in a group counseling session, "My wife thinks I'm too nosy. I know it's true because that's what she keeps writing in her diary."

Keep your eyes wide open before you marry, and then close them just a little bit after you are married.

Learn how to talk things out in the spirit of love. If you decide not to spend time and talk to your wife, remember the lesson from Adam, the first man.

Adam discovered that if he did not talk to Eve, his wife, the Devil would. Look at the trouble that followed.

(46) Ephesians 5:25 & Colossians 3:19

★ ★ ★ ★ ★

SHARE WITH OTHERS HOW TO GO TO HEAVEN

Let me ask you a very important question. Are you 100% sure you are going to heaven when you die?

The Bible says that God is *"not willing that any should perish, but that all should come to repentance"* II Peter 3:9. In other words, God wants everyone, including you, to go to Heaven when they die.

You may ask, "How can I know now that I will go to Heaven when I die?"

Jesus came down from Heaven to make it possible for us to go to Heaven. He said, *"I am the way, the truth, and the life: no man cometh unto the Father, but by me."* John 14:6.

When He was here, He told us how to go there (Heaven). Here is what He said, *"For God so loved the world, that He gave His only begotten Son, that whosoever believeth in Him should not perish, but have everlasting life."* John 3:16.

★ ★ ★ ★ ★   41

God wants you to know that you are loved.

The Lord Jesus said, *"For God so loved the world"* You are a part of this world, and God loves you. He gave His Son for you, and He wants you *"to know the love of Christ"* Ephesians 3: 19.

God wants you to know that you are of worth.

We are so dear to God *"that He gave His only begotten Son"* The Bible teaches us that we are all sinners. *"For all have sinned and come short of the glory of God."* Romans 3:23. The Bible teaches us that *"the wages of sin is death."* Romans 6:23.

The Bible also teaches us that *"Christ died for our sins according to the scriptures."* I Corinthians 15:3. God demonstrated His love for us and our worth to Him when He sent His Son to die in our place.

The good news is that the Lord Jesus paid our sin debt in full when He died on the cross. The Bible says, *"For he hath made him to be sin for us, who knew no sin; that we might be made the righteousness of God in him."* II Corinthians 5:21.

Christ loved us and gave Himself for us as payment for our sin. You may ask, *"How can God forgive my sin?"* He can because of what Jesus did. *"While we were yet sinners, Christ died for us."* Romans 5:8. He died for you.

God wants you to know that you can have hope.

He said, *"that whosoever believeth in Him should not perish."* Life is fragile, and people are perishing, but Christ came *"that they might have life, and that they might have it more abundantly."* John 10:10. In a world where so many have lost hope,

God wants us to know that the *"Lord Jesus Christ...is our hope"* I Timothy 1:1. He rose from the dead, and He said, *"Because **I** live, **ye** shall live also."* John 14:19.

God wants you to know that you can have purpose.

He desires that we *"should not perish but have everlasting life."* *"And this is the promise that He hath promised us, even eternal life."* I John 2:25. You may ask, "How can **I** receive God's promise of eternal life?"

Acknowledge that you are a sinner, *"for all have sinned, and come short of the glory of God."* Romans 3:23.

Believe that the Lord Jesus died for you, for *"Christ died for our sins according to the scriptures."* I Corinthians 15:3.

Call upon the Lord to save you, *"for whosoever shall call upon the name of the Lord shall be saved."* Romans 10:13. If you would be willing to turn to Christ in repentance and faith, pray this simple prayer of salvation:

★ ★ ★ ★ ★

LORD, I know that I am a sinner, and I believe You died and rose again for me. I trust You to forgive me. Come into my heart and save me. Help me to live for You. In Jesus' name, Amen.

The Lord Jesus said, *"...I give unto them eternal life; and they shall never perish."* John 10:28.

Everlasting life is ours when we receive Christ as our personal Saviour.

All Scripture taken from the Authorized Version

(1) Proverbs 18:22 (2) III John 1:4 (3) Ephesians 5:31, 32 (4) Psalms 62:8 (5) Psalm 62:8 (6) Proverbs 4:23) (7) Genesis 24:1-9 (8) John 8:29 (9) I Thessalonians 5:22 (10) Ephesians 5:25 (11) Ephesians 6: 1-3 (12) I Corinthians 13:11 (13) I Timothy 5:14 (14) Proverbs 21:9,19 (15) I Timothy 5:8 (16) Genesis 2:24 (17) Matthew 19: 4-6 (18) Matthew 24:43 (19) Hebrews 13:7,17 (20) John 14:2-3 (21) II Corinthians 6:14(22) Hebrews 12: 1- 2 (23) Ecclesiastes 7:8 (24) John 2: 1, 2 (25) Proverbs 17:17 (26) Proverbs 27:6 (27) Proverbs 13:20 (28) Psalm 37: 3-5 (29) Psalm 84:11 (30) Proverbs 18:22 (31) Romans 1:17 (32) I Peter 1:4 (33) Romans 12:2 (34) Philippians 3:13,14 (35) John 8:2-11 (36) Philippians 4:6-7 (37) Matthew 19:1-8 (38) Psalm 127:1 (39) I John 1:9 (40) John 8:29 (41) Ephesians 5:19 & 21 (42) Proverbs 18:21 (43) Proverbs 17:28 (44) Luke 22:32 (45) Proverbs 13:20, 27:17 (46) Ephesians 5:25 & Colossians 3:19

WordToTheWorld@aol.com

www.FiveStarChristianMinistries.com

www.ingramcontent.com/pod-product-compliance
Lightning Source LLC
Chambersburg PA
CBHW052123030426
42335CB00025B/3092